DesOps: Prepare Today for the Future of Design!

(Handout Version of the Slides)

Samir Dash

desops.io
2018

DesOps: Prepare Today for the Future of Design!
(Handout Version of the Slides)

desops.io

his book is a handout version of the deck used in the
workshop on DesOps conducted on 5th August 2018, at
DevConf India 2008 Conference.

For more information about the event, visit:

**http://desops.io/2018/07/04/talk-at-devconf18-
designops-prepare-today-for-future-of-design/**

This book is provided at the cost of production,
without any profit to the author. The electronic
version of this book is freely available online at
desops.io and related sites.

DesOps
Design Operations

Prepare Today for the Future of Design! v12

SAMIR DASH
Principal Software Engineer (UX), Red Hat

05 AUG 2018

DEVCONF.IN

redhat. CHRIST fedora

Most people make the mistake of thinking design is what it looks like. [...] It's not just what it looks like and feels like.

DESIGN is how it works.

"

DESIGN .is creative problem Solving.

Every role **.is** a DESIGNer role.

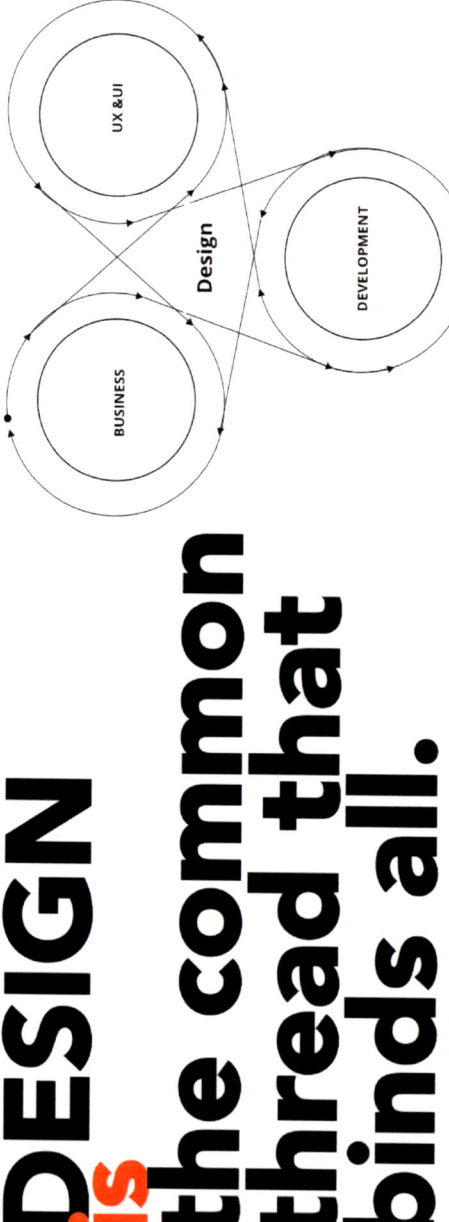

DESIGN is the common thread that binds all.

Every organization is a DESIGN organization.

Organization operations *are* a fabric of feedback-loops.

DesOps
helps
in finding
& enabling
shortest & most
effective
feedback-loop.

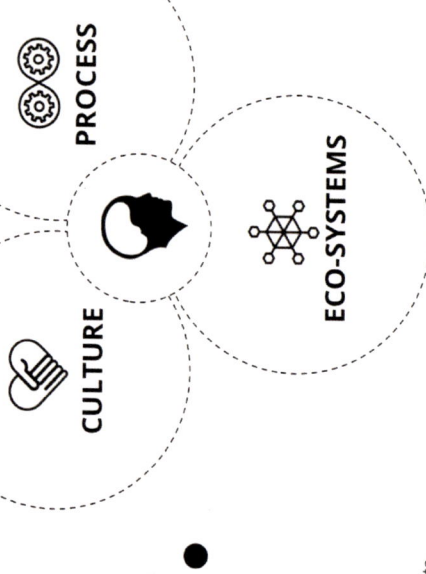

DesOps is a mindset.

...and a **belief-system** to empower the enterprise with the culture, processes and eco-systems to support design-driven process and data-driven decision making with agility and speed to conceptualize and deliver great products.

PROCESS

CULTURE

ECO-SYSTEMS

DesOps is inspired from DevOps mindset.

- a mindset
- remove waste
- define repeatable, reliable process
- automate
- enable feedback-loops
- be lean

DesOps helps take next-steps for DevOps.

- no more limited to dev2deploy cycle
- connect vision to delivered value
- cover whole lifecycle
- End to End Feedback loops
- handle human aspects
- bring design-thinking as way of life
- prefer 'outcome' over 'output'

Left-to-right brain analogy

Code Quality Checks

Customer Validations

API-UI Functional Bugs

Backend Functional Issues

User Testing

A/B or Split Testing

API Issues

UI/Front-end Bug

Cosmetic Issues

Usability Issues

Explorative Testing

End-user Feedback

Data Testing

Code Optimization Checks

Backend Issues

Accessibility Issues

Bug Reporting

EMOTIONAL

LOGICAL

$$\nabla \xi \frac{\partial \gamma}{\partial p} + \nabla_A \frac{\partial \gamma}{\partial q} = 0$$

$$dr = \frac{\Phi|\beta|W}{(2\pi)^{3}c^{2}} \left| c d\Sigma + \mathbf{b} \frac{\partial \Sigma}{\partial z} A d\dot{\xi} \right|$$

$$\Delta x = v_i \cdot t + \frac{1}{2} a t^2$$

DesOps=DevOps 2.0

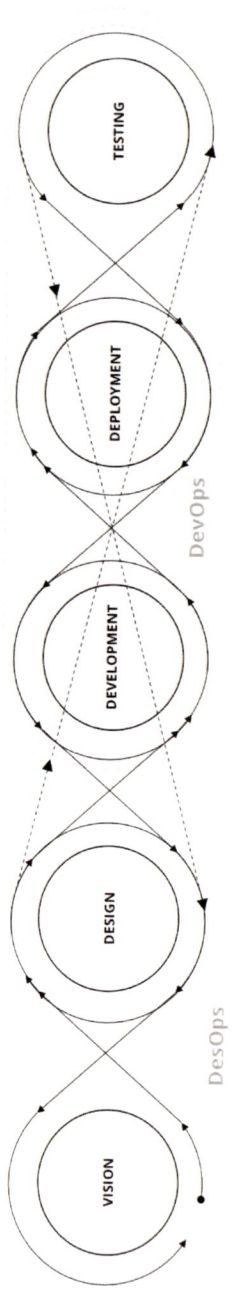

VISION · DESIGN · DEVELOPMENT · DEPLOYMENT · TESTING

DesOps · DevOps

So Where to Start?

STEP 1.

PROCESS

First step in DesOps is to discover touch-points.

STEP**1**

To achieve this **apply** DesignThinking as the way of life.

Ontology
of touch-points.

Read more

Role - Role

Theory/Discipline - Theory/Discipline

Role - Theory/Discipline

Theory/Discipline - Model/Framework

Discipline - Method

Tool /Technique - Instrument/System

Method - Tool/Technique

Role - Instrument/System

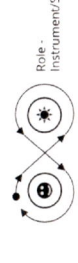

'Petals Process Diagram' (PPD) is about discovery of touch-points.

- Easy Visualization
- Atomic Level
- Feedback-loops
- Touch Points
- Decision Points

PRM

MR

PM

QA

DEP

ARC

DBA

Read more about Petals Process Diagram

http://desops.io/2018/06/07/paperback-the-desops-enterprise-re-invent-your-organization-volume-1-the-overview-culture/

STEP1

PPD.

STEP1

The Feedback-loop between the *Product Manager* and the *Interaction Designer*.

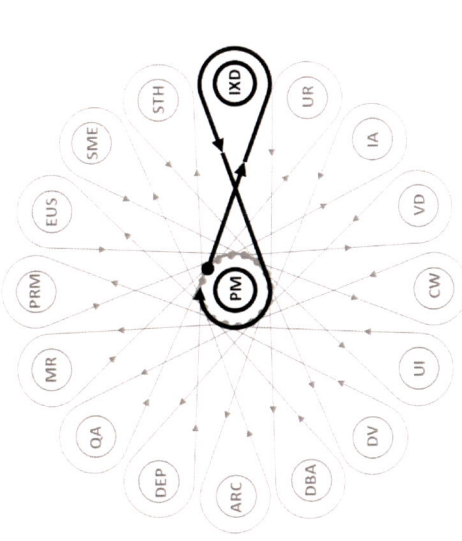

- PM - Product Manager / Product Owner
- PRM - Project Manager / Scrum Master
- SME - Subject Matter Expert
- STH - Stake Holders / Client / Product Owner / Investor / CEO / Program Manager
- MR - Market Researcher / Market Analyst / Business Analyst
- QA - Quality Assurance Member / Tester
- DEP - Deployment Expert / CI CD Expert / Infrastructure / Storage / Container Management / Server Management etc.
- ARC - Architect , Technical Lead

- UI - Frontend Developer / HTML CSS Expert / Flash ActionScript Coder / Rich Media Developer / iOS, Android Studio Developers / Native Application and Apps developer / Widget Creator / Interactive Prototyper etc.
- DBA - Database Admin / Data Migration Specialist / Data Architect / Big Data, Hadoop Experts DV - Backend Developer / API Developer / Micro Services Coder etc.
- VD - Visual Designer / Visual Asset creator / Special Effects Designer / Visual Story Board Designer / Audio Visual Expert
- CW - Story writer / User narrative Maker / Content writer
- IXD - Interaction Designer / Experience Designer
- IA - Information Architect / Customer experience dinagner / Usability Expert
- UR - User Research Expert / Usability Tester

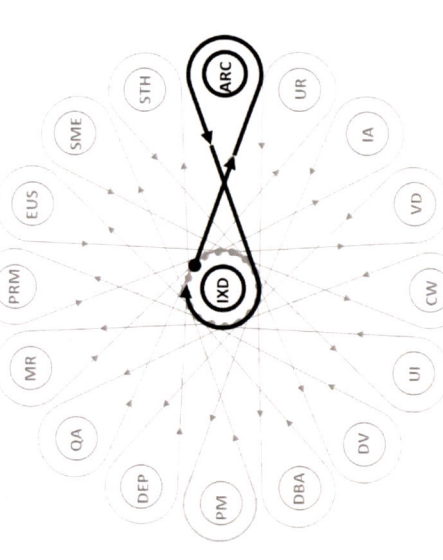

The follow up
Feedback-loop between
the *Interaction Designer*
with a *Technical Architect*.

STEP1

- PM - Product Manager / Product Owner
- PRM - Project Manager / Scrum Master
- SME - Subject Matter Expert
- STH - Stake Holders / Client / Product Owner / Inventor/ CEO / Program Manager
- MR - Market Researcher / Market Analyst / Business Analyst
- QA - Quality Assurance Member / Tester
- DEP - Deployment Expert / CI CD Expert / Infrastructure / Storage / Container Management / Server Management etc.
- ARC - Architect - Technical Lead

- UI - Frontend Developer / HTML CSS Expert / Flash ActionScript Coder / Rich Media Developer / iOS, Android Studio Developers/ Native Application and Apps developers / Widget Creator / Interactive Prototypers etc.
- DBA - Database Admin / Data Migration Specialist / Data Architect / Big Data, Hadoop Experts DV   Backend Developer / API Developer/ Micro Services Coder etc.
- VD - Visual Designer / Visual Asset creator / Special Effects Designer / Visual Story Board Designer / Audio Visual Expert
- CW - Story writer / User narrative Maker / Content writer
- IXD - Interaction Designer / Experience Designer
- IA - Information Architect / Customer experience designer / Usability Expert
- UR - User Research Expert / Usability Tester

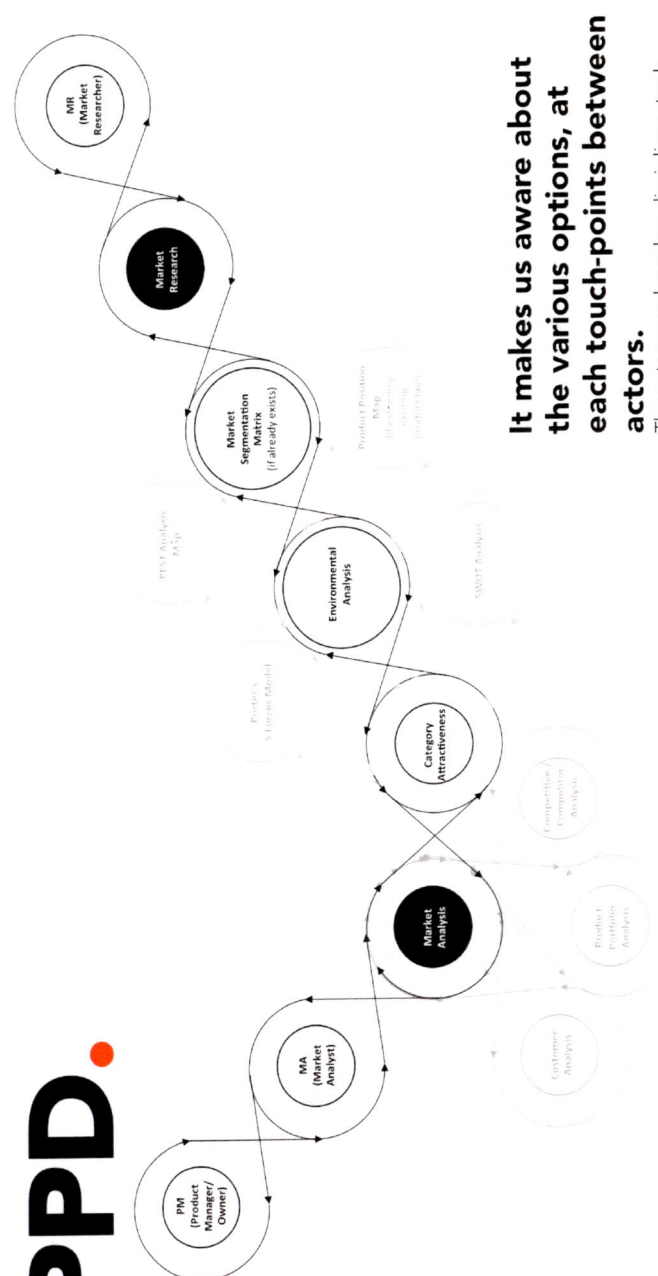

PPD.

STEP1

It makes us aware about the various options, at each touch-points between actors.

The actors can be roles, disciplines, tools technologies, models, methodologies or even practices involved in that process.

PPD.

STEP1

Easier way to draw the PPD.

PM (Product Manager/Owner)

MA (Market Analyst)

Market Analysis

Customer Analysis

Product Portfolio Analysis

Competitor / Competitor Analysis

Category Attractiveness

Porter's 5 Forces Model

Environmental Analysis

PEST Analysis Map

Product Position Map (if extending existing product line)

SWOT Analysis

Market Segmentation Matrix (if already exists)

Market Research

MR (Market Researcher)

Used Path in the Scenario

Potential Path in the Scenario

STEP1

Example #1 Optimizing, Automating & Reducing Touch Points

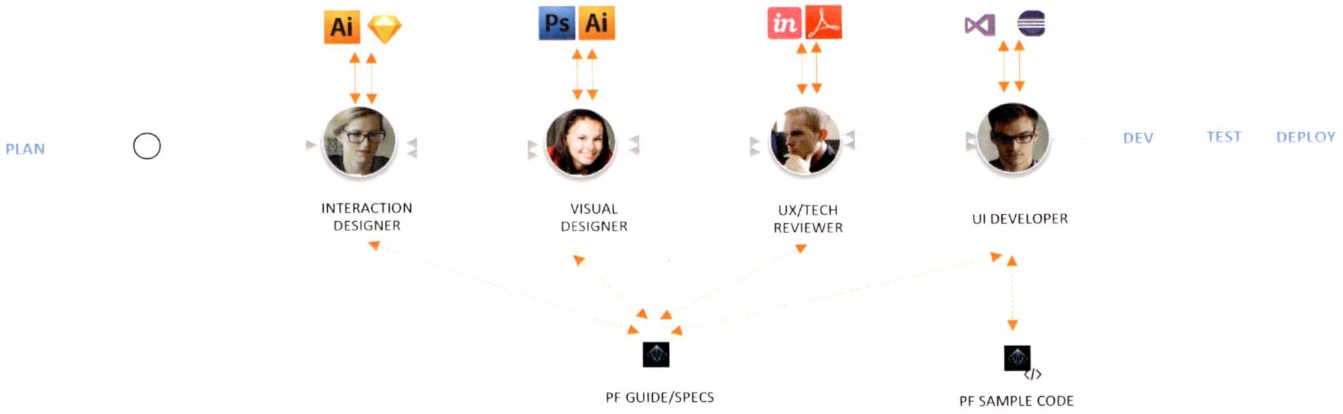

PLAN   DEV   TEST   DEPLOY

INTERACTION DESIGNER   VISUAL DESIGNER   UX/TECH REVIEWER   UI DEVELOPER

PF GUIDE/SPECS   PF SAMPLE CODE

KNOW Ditto – Design Life Cycle Management Concept
MORE http://desops.io/2018/05/12/slides-ditto-design-life-cycle-management-concept-for-desops-2016-12/

Translating Value at Different Stages of Design with Minimal Waste
http://desops.io/2018/05/12/translating-value-at-different-stages-of-design-with-minimal-waste/

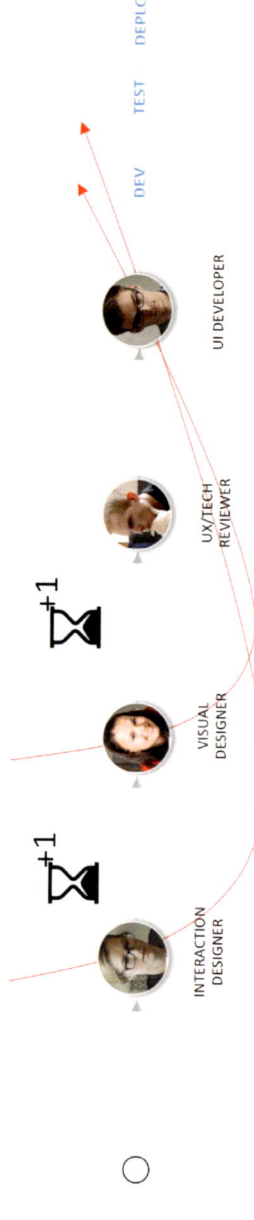

Example #1

Optimizing, Automating & Reducing Touch Points

STEP1

PLAN   DEV   TEST   DEPLOY

INTERACTION DESIGNER

VISUAL DESIGNER

UX/TECH REVIEWER

UI DEVELOPER

+1   +1

KNOW MORE

Ditto – Design Life Cycle Management Concept
http://desops.io/2018/05/12/slides-ditto-design-life-cycle-management-concept-for-desops-2016-17/

Translating Value at Different Stages of Design with Minimal Waste
http://desops.io/2018/05/12/translating-value-at-different-stages-of-design-with-minimal-waste/

STEP2.

ECO-SYSTEM

Enable through the acts of

Optimize what is happening around a touch-point.

Automate & remove manual / repeatable interventions across touch-point.

Reduce the number of touch-points in a process, using process redesign and new work practices, and enabling through technology.

STEP2

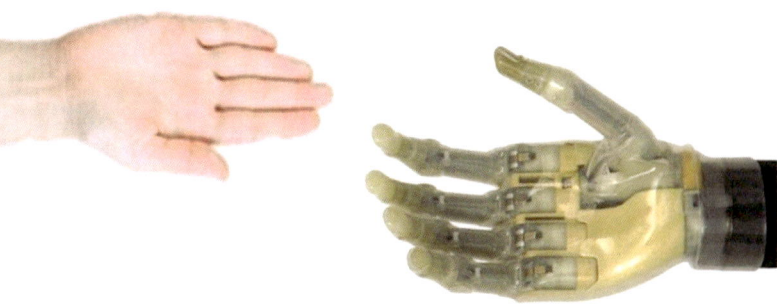

Next... enable touch-points **with** more efficient bionic parts!

STEP2

STEP 2

Example #1 Optimizing, Automating & Reducing Touch Points

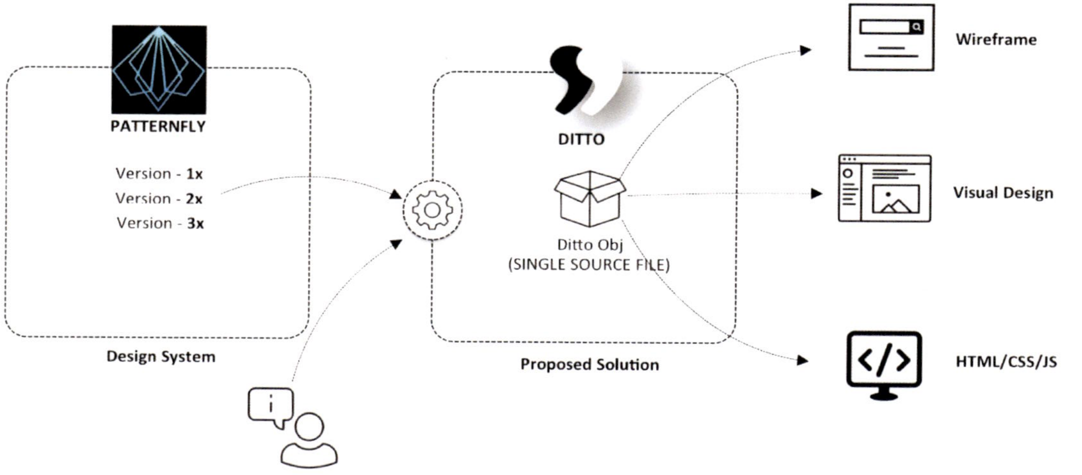

Wireframe

Visual Design

HTML/CSS/JS

DITTO

Ditto Obj
(SINGLE SOURCE FILE)

Proposed Solution

PATTERNFLY

Version - 1x
Version - 2x
Version - 3x

Design System

KNOW **Ditto – Design Life Cycle Management Concept**
MORE http://desops.io/2018/05/12/slides-ditto-design-life-cycle-management-concept-for-desops-2016-17/

Translating Value at Different Stages of Design with Minimal Waste
http://desops.io/2018/05/12/translating-value-at-different-stages-of-design-with-minimal-waste/

Example #1

Optimizing, Automating & Reducing Touch Points

STEP2

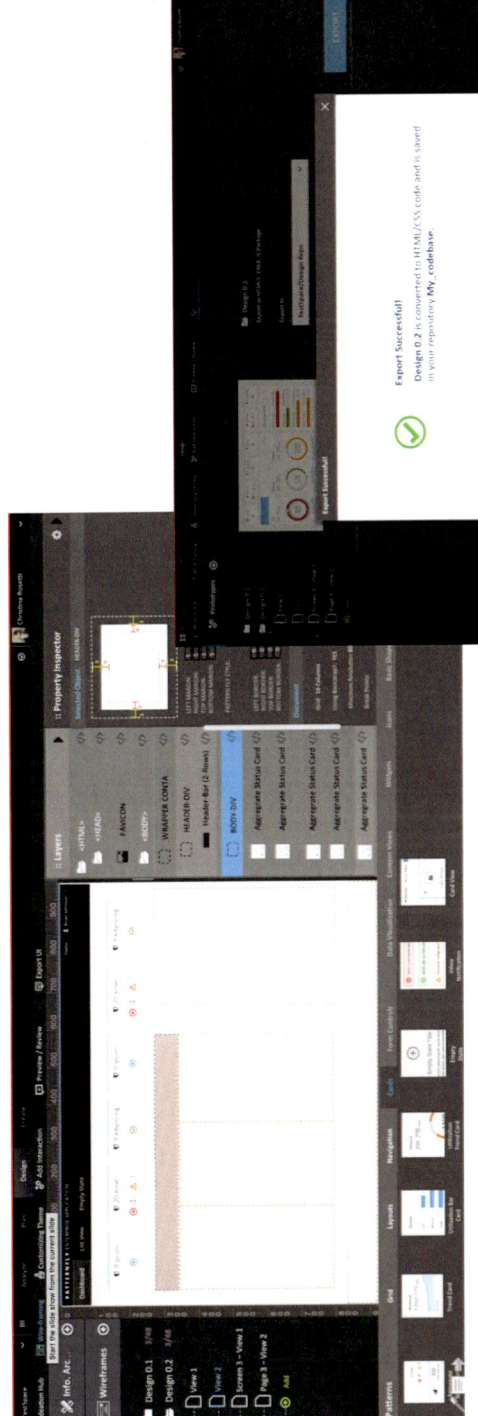

KNOW Ditto – Design Life Cycle Management Concept
MORE http://desops.io/2018/05/12/slides-ditto-design-life-cycle-management-concept-for-desops-2016-17/

Translating Value at Different Stages of Design with Minimal Waste
http://desops.io/2018/05/12/translating-value-at-different-stages-of-design-with-minimal-waste/

Example #1 Optimizing, Automating & Reducing Touch Points

DEMO.

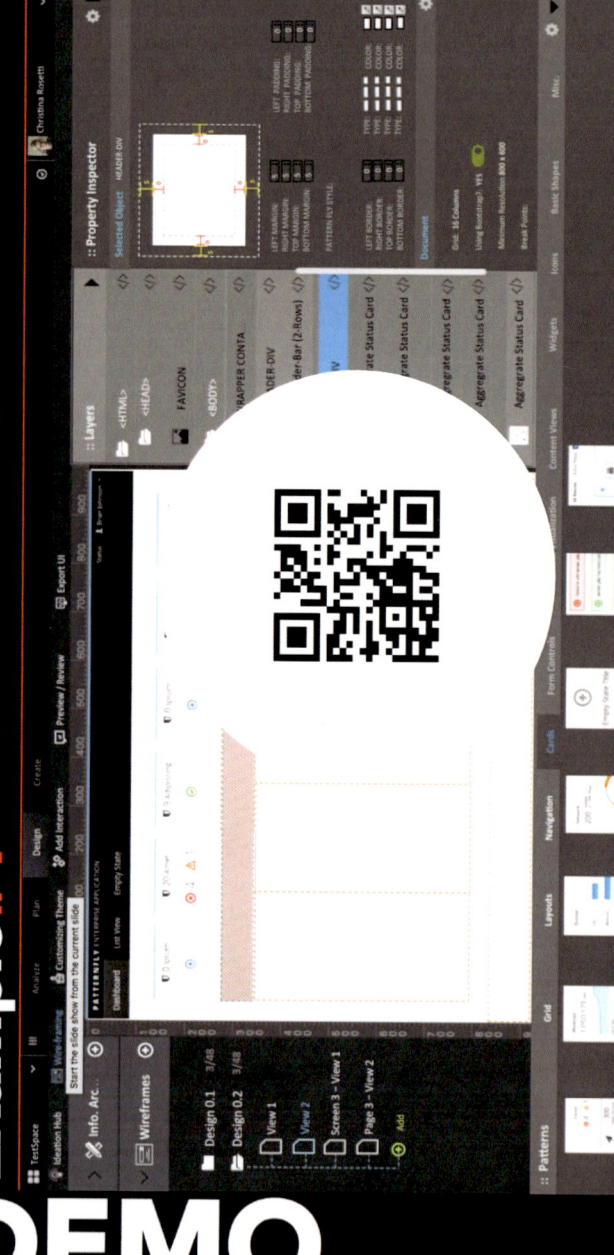

Ditto

KNOW MORE

Ditto – Design Life Cycle Management Concept
http://desops.io/2018/05/12/slides-ditto-a-design-life-cycle-management-concept-for-desops-2016-17/

Translating Value at Different Stages of Design with Minimal Waste
http://desops.io/2018/05/12/translating-value-at-different-stages-of-design-with-minimal-waste/

Example #2

Building Loop Between Design with Testing

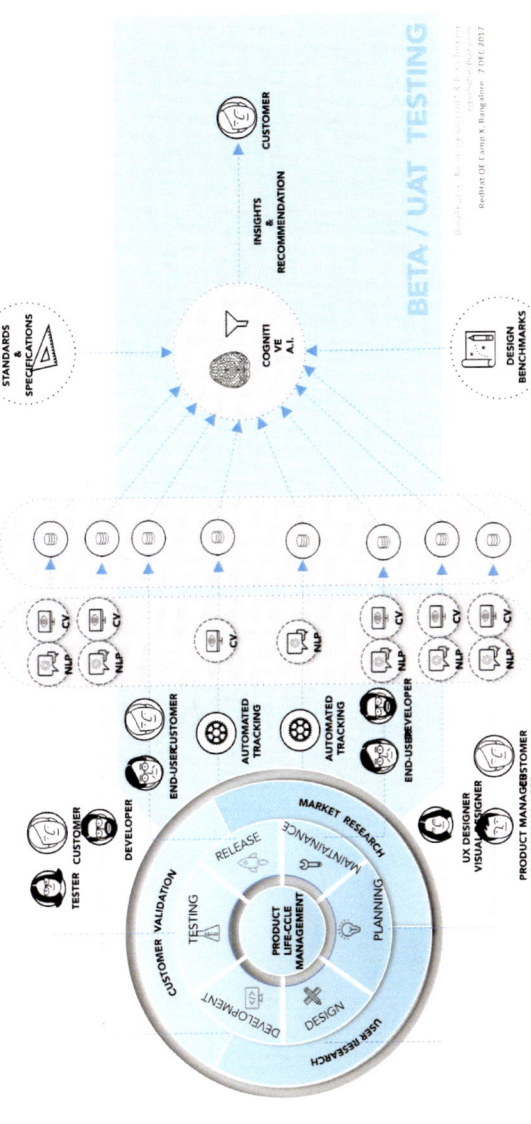

BETA / UAT TESTING

STANDARDS & SPECIFICATIONS

COGNITIVE A.I.

INSIGHTS & RECOMMENDATION

CUSTOMER

DESIGN BENCHMARKS

TESTER CUSTOMER

DEVELOPER

END-USER CUSTOMER

AUTOMATED TRACKING

AUTOMATED TRACKING

END-USER DEVELOPER

UX DESIGNER
VISUAL DESIGNER
PRODUCT MANAGER CUSTOMER MANAGER
PRODUCT MANAGER PROJECT MANAGER

NLP CV
NLP CV
CV
NLP
NLP CV
NLP CV

CUSTOMER VALIDATION
RELEASE
TESTING
PRODUCT LIFE-CLCLE MANAGEMENT
DEVELOPMENT
DESIGN
PLANNING
MAINTAINANCE
MARKET RESEARCH
USER RESEARCH

KNOW BetaStudio - RedHat Idea-Incubation - 2017   **Re-imagining beta testing in the ever-changing world of automation**
MORE https://youtu.be/kItaD5wc4_4   https://opensource.com/article/18/1/beta-testing-automation

Example #2
Building Loop Between Design with Testing

DESIGN BENCHMARKS — Collect Benchmark data from design stage

AUTOMATED TRACKING — Track & Collect data from product

FEEDBACK & USER TESTING — Data from User feedback & User Testing

STANDARDS & SPECIFICATIONS — Collect Standards & Specifications

COMPUTER VISION NLP — Process Unstructured data to get inference

MODEL & METRICS — Model the data and Map against the Metrics

A.I. & COGNITIVE — AI helps finding the outliers & generate Insights / recommendations

Spectra POC
Auto Generate Design Specification from Any Design files

betaStudio POC
{css} {JS}

In-App Tracking POC

Pattern-AI POC

Web Content Accessibility Guideline (WCAG) Section 508
Web Accessibility Initiative Spec,
ARIA Design Principles,
W3C Compliance

JS Standards

CSS Standards & Grids
Code Optimization Metrics
Error codes & Specs
Device Specific Guidelines (e.g.
Apple Human Interface Guideline)
...

KNOW MORE

BetaStudio - RedHat Idea-Incubation - 2017 https://youtu.be/kitoD5wc4_4

Re-imagining beta testing in the ever-changing world of automation https://opensource.com/article/18/1/beta-testing-automation

Spectra 2.0 : My Experiments in Cloud Based Design Process Automation http://dtsops.io/2018/05/07/spectra-2.0-my-experiments-in-cloud-based-design-process-automation/

RedHat UX Camp X Bangalore 7/8E 2017

Example #2.1

Building Loop Between Design with Testing

Spec*****tra

helps in collect benchmark data from design stage.

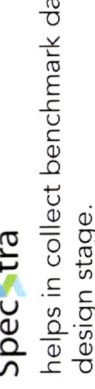

SAMPLE GENERATED GUIDE

https://
samirshomepage.files.wordpress.com/
2016/08/sample-generated-style-guide-
outout1418308769-en.pdf

Spectra 2.0 : My Experiments in Cloud Based Design Process Automation

http://desops.io/2018/05/07/spectra-2-0-my-experiments-in-
cloud-based-design-process-automation/

**KNOW
MORE**

Text & Font Usage Overview

Total Text Objects Found: 7
Total Embedded Fonts Used: 2
Name of Fonts Used:

1. Roboto-Thin
2. Roboto-R . . . .

Design File Overview

File Type: ai
File Name: freshbui
File Size: 92.37 KB
Upload date: December 11, 2014, 2:39 pm
Design File Creator: Adobe Illustrator 156 (Windows)

Creation Date: 08/27/14 18:26:55
Last Modified: 08/27/14 18:26:55

AIX Version: 1.5
Page Dimension: 1440 x 2560 px
Page Size: 1080 x 1920 pts
File Size: 92.37 KB

Encryption: no
Optimisation: no

Actual Used Color Palette:

Text [Text 1]

Textbox Content
Bloodpressure(mmHg)

Textbox Dimensions :
Width : 824px (Screen Pixel)
Height : 105.33px (Screen Pixel)

Width : 618pt
Height : 79pt

Absolute Position :
Left : 308px (Screen Pixel)
Top : 888px (Screen Pixel)

Left : 231pt
Top : 666pt

Font Formatting :
Font Name: Roboto-Thin
Font Size: 60 pt
Font Style:
Font Color: #ffffff

Misc :

Total Font Colo
Name of Font C

1. #ffffff
2. #2a...

Rendered Image – R

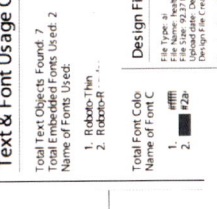

Total Colors Used: 46
Total Web-safe Colors Used: 12
Web-safe Colors Compatibly: 2X

Most Used Resultant Color Palet

#1EC3B3
#FFFFFF
#2A4043
#B3B3B3
#808080
#C3EFEA
#96E3DC
#3BD3C7
#2EC7B8
#19F6FA

Actual Used Color Palette: (HEX)

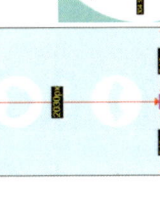
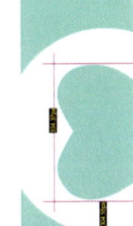

Specstra

Example #2.1 Building Loop Between Design and Testing

DEMO.

Specstra 2.0 : My Experiments in Cloud Based Design Process Automation
http://desops.io/2018/05/07/specstra-2-0-my-experiments-in-
cloud-based-design-process-automation/

KNOW
MORE

Example #2.2

Building Loop Between Design with Testing

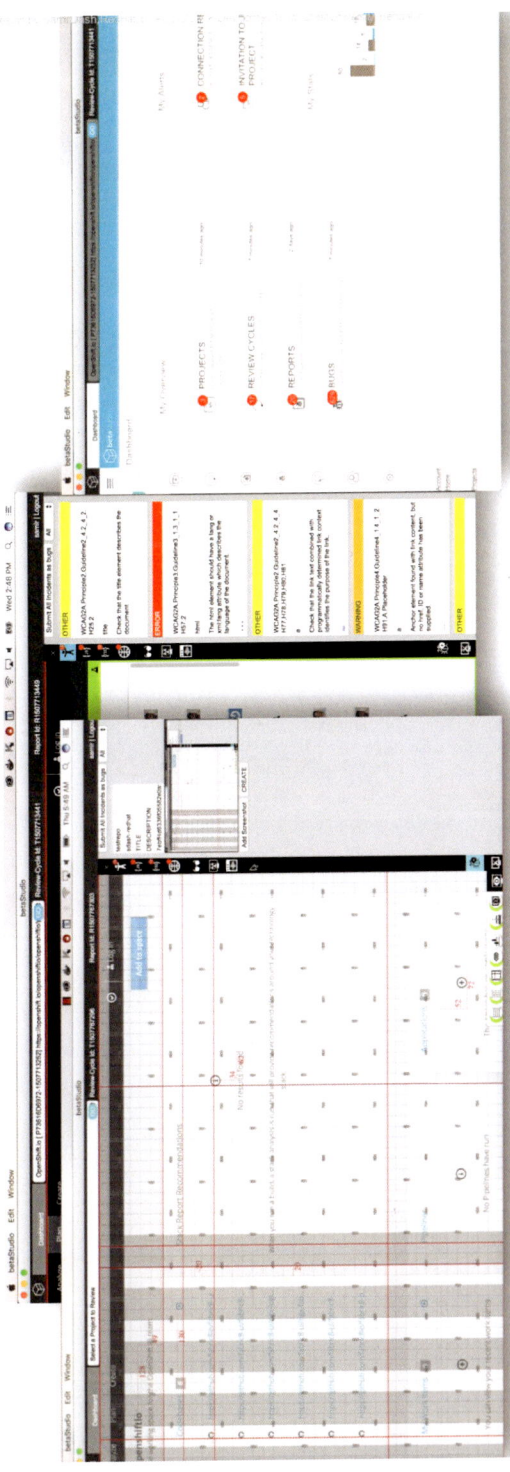

KNOW MORE

Re-imagining beta testing in the ever-changing world of automation
https://opensource.com/article/18/7/beta-testing-automation

BetaStudio - RedHat Idea-Incubation - 2017
https://youtu.be/kIuoD5wc4_4

BetaStudio

Example #2.2 Building Loop Between Design and Testing

DEMO.

Re-imagining beta testing in the ever-changing world of automation
https://opensource.com/article/18/1/beta-testing-automation

BetaStudio - RedHat Idea-Incubation - 2017
https://youtu.be/XitqDbxvd_A

CULTURE

Is the
Organization
is culturally
ready?

DesOps Culture is about ...

Innovation Fuelling
parenting innovation from
Adopting grassroots
Diversity Open to
Collaborative Feedback
decision making
Design Thinking take risk
as a way of life.

Freedom to
explore,
to innovate
Zero biased
mindsets

DesOps
Organization
is essentially
Open
Organization.

THE OPEN
ORGANIZATION
IGNITING PASSION AND PERFORMANCE

JIM WHITEHURST
CEO, RED HAT

WITH A FOREWORD BY GARY HAMEL

The Open Organization by Jim Whitehurst
https://www.redhat.com/en/explore/
the-open-organization-book

DesOps Culture is Essentially a Culture of the Open Organization
https://www.linkedin.com/pulse/desops-culture-essentially-open-
organization-samir-dash/

http://desops.io/2018/06/07/paperback-the-desops-
enterprise-re-invent-your-organization-volume-1-the-
overview-culture/

Actually setting up the right culture is the

STEP 0.

CULTURE

KNOW
MORE

DesOps – (Design Operations) Articles
http://desops.io/desops-design-operations/

The DesOps Enterprise : Volume1 - Overview & Culture by Samir Dash
http://desops.io/2018/06/07/paperback-the-desops-enterprise-re-invent-your-organization-volume-1-the-overview-culture/

So to prepare for the future of design …

STEP0
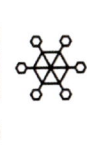
CULTURE

STEP1
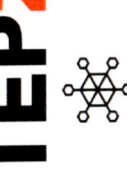
PROCESS

STEP2

ECO-SYSTEMS

Thank U.

Be in touch!

twitter: @mobilewish

Explore more at

www.ingramcontent.com/pod-product-compliance
Lightning Source LLC
Chambersburg PA
CBRC100755170526
45159CB00011B/3098